ACTION DUDE

WRITTEN + DRAWN BY
ANDY RILEY

WELBECK
FLAME

FIRST PUBLISHED IN 2022 BY WELBECK FLAME
AN IMPRINT OF WELBECK CHILDREN'S LIMITED,
PART OF WELBECK PUBLISHING GROUP.
BASED IN LONDON AND SYDNEY.
WWW.WELBECKPUBLISHING.COM

ISBN: 978 1 80130 014 8

PRINTED IN CHINA

10 9 8 7 6 5 4 3 2 1

MIX
Paper from
responsible sources
FSC® C144853

ACTIONDUDE.CO.UK

CHAPTER ONE

HEY. MEET ACTION DUDE

I AM **ACTION DUDE**.

THAT'S TOTALLY MY REAL NAME! IMAGINE THAT.

FIRST NAME... **ACTION.** SECOND NAME... **DUDE.**

ACTION DUDE.

NOT **CHARLIE.** I'M NOT CHARLIE, NEVER CALL ME CHARLIE, I DON'T EVEN KNOW WHY I **SAID** CHARLIE JUST THEN.

LOOK AT MY BIG MUSCLY ARMS.

ARMS BUILT FOR ACTION!

YOU DIDN'T LOOK AT THEM FOR LONG ENOUGH.

LOOK AGAIN PLEASE.

THANK YOU!

FLEX FLEX FLEX

I ONCE CRASHED A DIGGER INTO A SHIP AND RODE A BIKE INTO A TORNADO *ON THE SAME DAY!*

AND THERE'S *TONS* AND *TONS* OF OTHER THINGS...

CHARLIE!

I USED MY **TROUSERS** TO STOP AN **AVALANCHE!**

LIKE I WAS SAYING...

CHARLIE!

≥ SIGH ≤ WHAT IS IT, MUM?

WE NEED MILK AND BREAD.

CHARLIE'S NOT MY NAME. I CHANGED MY NAME, DIDN'T I. LOOK AT THE CARD.

OH, THAT'S RIGHT.

THE CARD.

OFFICIAL HERO ID CARD

1ST NAME: ACTION
2ND NAME: DUDE

ONLY DANGEROUS JOBS ACCEPTED

7

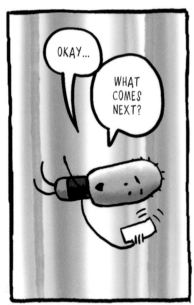

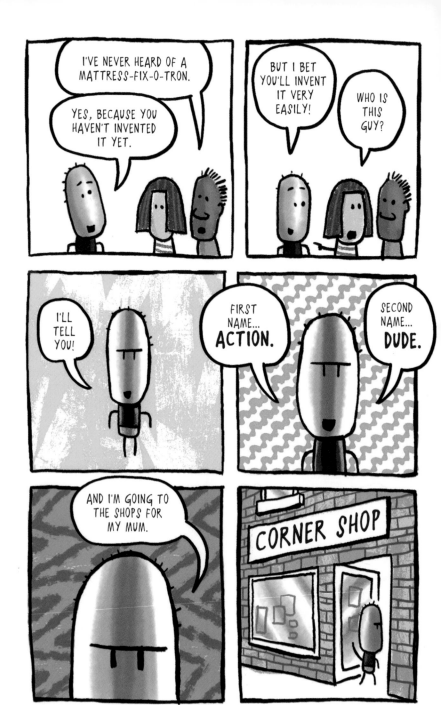

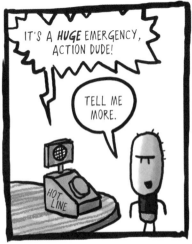

15

YOU KNOW THAT NEW THEME PARK OUTSIDE TOWN?

YEP. **PREHISTORIC LAND.**

WE GOT A FLYER THROUGH THE DOOR. "MEET MAMMOTHS, CAVE PEOPLE AND SABRE-TOOTHED TIGERS... BUT ALL ROBOTS, AND ALL PERFECTLY SAFE, IN THIS RECREATION OF THE STONE-AGE WORLD."

SOUNDS COOL.

WELL, THOSE "SAFE ROBOTS" HAVE TURNED **HOSTILE!** THEY'RE ATTACKING THE GUESTS!

THERE'S PEOPLE TRAPPED IN THE THEME PARK AND THEY NEED SOMEONE TO SAVE THEM!

PET TH HARMLE SABRE TOOTHED TIGERS!

Q: ARE OUR THEME PARK ROBOTS DANGEROUS IN ANY WAY?

A: NO!

MEET THE NO-THREAT CAVE PEOPLE

RISK=ZERO

DON'T MISS T FRIENDLY WO MAMMOT

17

CHAPTER TWO
GATEWAY TO PERIL

21

23

AND JUST LOOK AT THIS BRAVE POLICE HORSE.

MAGNIFICENT!

I HAVE ALL THIS STUFF BECAUSE **WE'RE THE POLICE.**

SO WHY DON'T I USE SOME OF THIS *POLICE* EQUIPMENT TO DO SOME POLICING? INSTEAD OF, YOU KNOW, JUST SENDING IN SOME KID?

I'LL FLY MY **QUADROCOPTER** IN THERE, AND THEN FLY EVERYONE OUT.

A POLICE RESCUE. BY THE POLICE. EVERYBODY GOT THAT?

MOMENTS LATER

BZZZZZ

BZZZZZ

BZZZZZ

BZZZZZZ

BZZZZZZ

27

TAKE A RADIO. I HOPE IT LASTS LONGER THAN NINA'S.

OOH. FREE RADIO!

WHO KNOWS WHAT DANGERS I WILL FACE...

WAIT!

WHY DON'T I COME TOO?

WILL I STILL GET TO DO SOME RUNNING, JUMPING AND BLOWING UP?

I KNOW PREHISTORIC LAND PRETTY WELL. I CAN HELP YOU.

WELL, YEAH.

NICE.

READY, CALLUM?

LET'S BOUNCE.

CHAPTER THREE
MONORAIL TO TERROR

THE MONORAIL WILL TAKE US DEEP INTO THE HEART OF THE PARK, ACTION DUDE.

FREE RADIO AND A FREE MONORAIL RIDE! TODAY KEEPS GETTING BETTER AND BETTER!

SO, HERE'S THE THING... THE ROBOTS DON'T KNOW THAT THEY **ARE** ROBOTS.

OH WELL THEN, THIS IS GOING TO BE EASY! WE JUST SAY, "HEY, YOU'RE ROBOTS, YOUR SETTINGS ARE WRONG, CALM DOWN."

31

38

39

AH RIGHT, **THAT'S WHY.**

I AM UGG OBOK!

LEADER OF UGG PEOPLE!

GREETINGS, I AM ACTION DUDE.

DO NOT SPEAK!

OKAY *SLIGHTLY* RUDE BUT WHATEVER.

41

CHAPTER FOUR
MASSIVE OPPONENT!

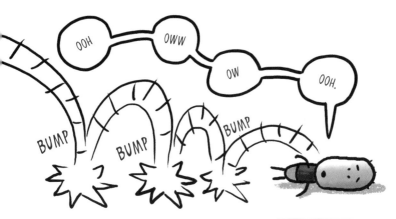

53

55

CHAPTER FIVE
DEADLY FELINE

ROAR!

HEY! THE ROAR BLEW THE SPIDER AWAY!

EVERYTHING'S GOING TO BE FINE!

OH NO, MY HEAD'S IN THE TIGER'S MOUTH.

WHICH IS CLOSING.

GRAB

GRAB

RUBY! WHILE I HOLD ITS TEETH...

LOOK FOR A BUTTON UNDER ITS LEG OR ARM OR WHATEVER...

MAKE ITS HEAD PING OFF...

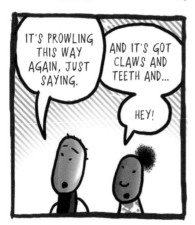

63

70

CHAPTER SIX

PARRRP!

PARRP

PAAAARP

PAARP

PAARRP

PARRPP

SOMETHING'S DEFINITELY GOING 'PARP.'

OOOH, RUBY, IT'S THE BIT WHERE THE RIDE GOES UP BEFORE IT DROPS US.

LOVE THIS PART!

CLANK

CLANK

BUT WHAT *IS* THAT PARP NOISE?

PARRRP

I DUNNO!

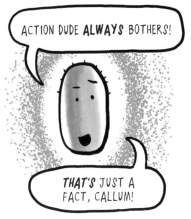

75

WE'RE FINE!

THANKS TO TOP QUALITY SEATBELTS.

👑

OFFICIAL ACTION DUDE SAFETY ADVICE

HEY, KIDS! WEAR A SEATBELT!

OKAY, THAT'S ENOUGH ADVICE.

ON WITH THE ACTION™.

I'M NOT CALLED **ADVICE DUDE**, AM I?

NINA'S CRASHED QUADROCOPTER.

NOBODY IN IT... BUT FOOTPRINTS LEADING TO...

CHAPTER SEVEN
INTO THE VOLCANO

83

AAAAARGH!

OKAY MY MISTAKE.

THAT IS TOTALLY REAL LAVA.

HOW TO GET OVER?

HMM.

DANGER DO NOT CROSS LAVA

I'M GOING TO USE THE 'DANGER DO NOT CROSS LAVA' SIGN AS A RAFT. TO CROSS THE LAVA!

WHAT DO WE THINK?

WELL, I KNOW YOU'LL DO IT WHATEVER I SAY, SO IT'LL SAVE TIME IF I JUST GO "SURE, GREAT PLAN".

YAY!

85

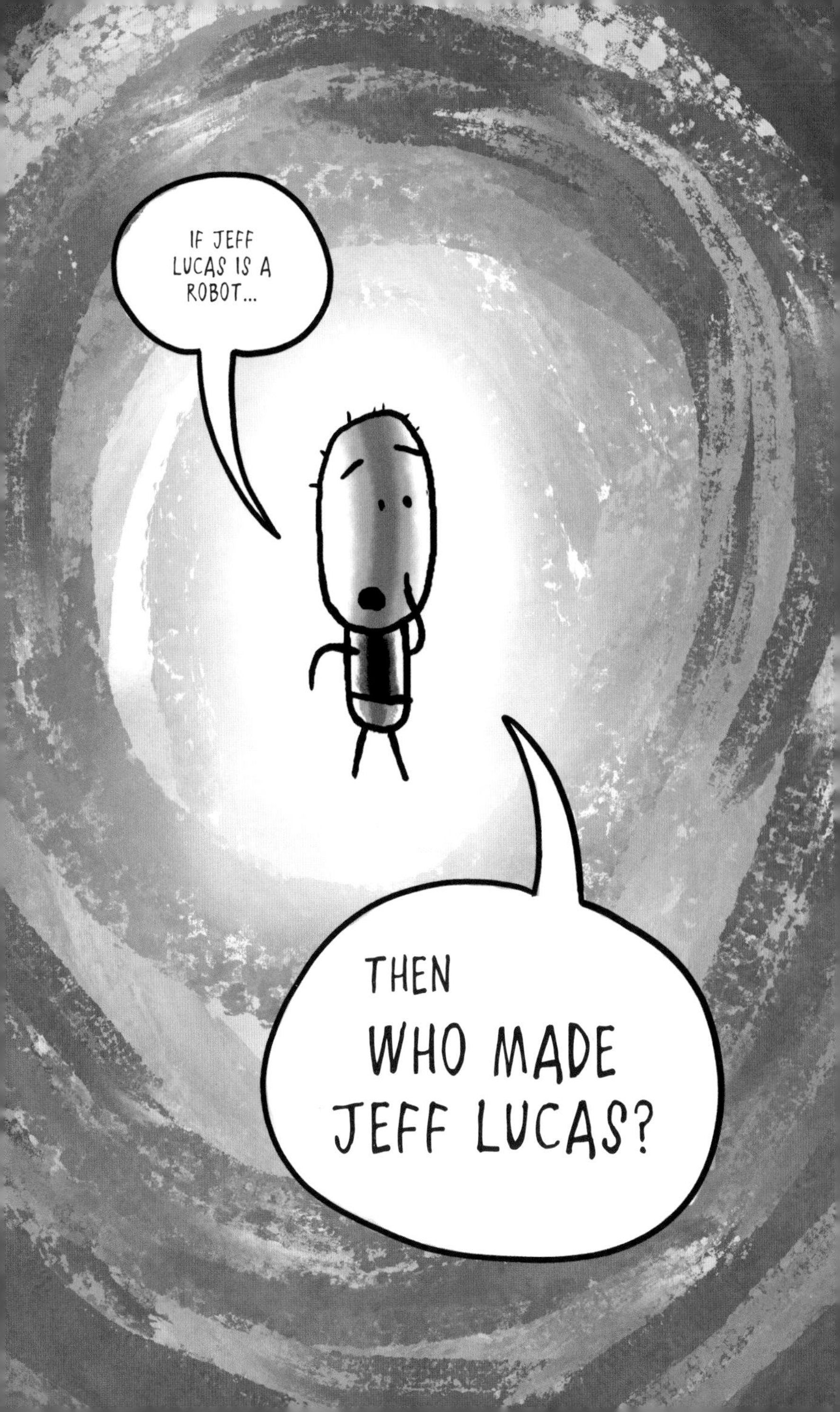
IF JEFF LUCAS IS A ROBOT...
THEN WHO MADE JEFF LUCAS?

CHAPTER EIGHT
THE PIT

GOT TO THINK.

NEVER LIKE TO SPEND *TOO* LONG THINKING.

THEY DON'T CALL ME **THOUGHT DUDE.**

BUT SOMETIMES IT HAS TO BE DONE.

PACE PACE PACE PACE

WHOEVER'S CONTROLLING IT ALL MUST BE SOMEONE WHO KNOWS THE PARK *REALLY WELL.*

PACE PACE

SOMEONE WHO...

HEY!

SUDDEN STOP

95

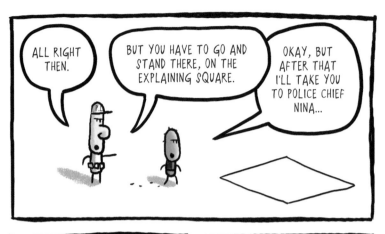

98

CHAPTER NINE
RAMPAGE

107

JUST WHEN I THOUGHT I'D WON!

HOW TOTALLY ANNOYING!

WHIZZ

NO TIME TO REST.

GOT TO FIND THE OTHERS!

MOMENTS LATER

SO ANYWAY, IT WAS **CALLUM ALL ALONG**! WHO WOULD HAVE THOUGHT? *UNBELIEVABLE!* ANYWAY, HE'S VERY CLEVER, TO BE FAIR, BUT ALSO KIND OF A *BAD PERSON* BECAUSE HE WANTS TO SELL HIS *POWERFUL ROBOTS* TO *ALL THE WORLD'S VILLAINS.*

OH YEAH, THE PARK'S TOTALLY CHILL NOW. THIS LITTLE PAD CONTROLS THE ROBOTS SO I SWIPED IT AND MADE THEM RELAX. SO I **WOULD** BE SAYING, PANIC'S OVER, EVERYTHING'S FINE, BUT HERE'S THE THING...

PREHISTORIC LAND MIGHT BE SAFE, BUT NOW IT'S **THE CITY** THAT'S IN DANGER!

I KNOW, RIGHT?

CALLUM'S STILL CONTROLLING *ONE ROBOT,* BUT IT'S THE *BIGGEST* ONE, THE PAD WON'T WORK ON IT, DON'T KNOW WHY, IT'S ON *MANUAL CONTROL* OR SOMETHING, AND WAIT AM I TALKING TOO MUCH? I'M TALKING TOO MUCH. I'M JUST A BIT PUMPED FROM ALL THE EXCITEMENT.

WOOP WOOP!

115

116

121

CHAPTER TEN
SAUSAGES FOR TEA

125

127

THE END

(FOR NOW...)

OKAY - GRAB A PEN AND PAPER, BECAUSE NOW WE'RE GOING TO LEARN HOW TO

DRAW ACTION DUDE WITH JUST TEN LINES!

THAT'S RIGHT **TEN LINES!** LET'S GO!

LINE 1:
DRAW A POTATO STANDING ON ITS END

LINE 2:
DRAW ANOTHER POTATO HIDING BEHIND THE FIRST ONE

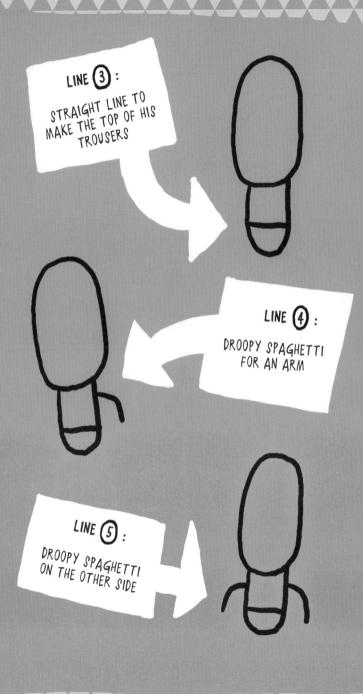

LINE **9** :
ANOTHER LITTLE DOT JUST HERE

LINE **10** :
A SMALL BANANA FOR A SMILE... AND **THAT'S IT!** YOU'VE DRAWN YOUR OWN **ACTION HERO!**
EASY WASN'T IT?

HE'S JUST A LITTLE POTATO-SPAGHETTI-BANANA GUY!

NOW WHY NOT DRAW HIM *RUNNING*... OR *JUMPING*... OR *SWIMMING*... OR *CLIMBING*...

ACTION DUDE CAN DO <u>ANYTHING!</u>

RUBY'S PAGE
WELL, I WASN'T GOING TO LET ACTION DUDE GET ALL THE BONUS PAGES, WAS I?

IF YOU ENJOYED THIS BOOK, DON'T
FORGET TO HAVE A LOOK AT...

ACTIONDUDE.CO.UK

THAT'S WHERE YOU CAN
DOWNLOAD A FEW
GOODIES LIKE THESE...

- FULL-COLOUR ACTION DUDE POSTER

- THE *ACTION DUDE* FONT
  (THIS ONE!) SO YOU CAN
  WRITE LIKE ACTION DUDE

- ACTIVITY SHEETS SO YOU
  CAN DRAW YOUR OWN ACTION
  DUDE STUNTS

- PICTURES AND POSTERS YOU
  CAN COLOUR IN YOURSELF

- PLUS: HOW TO CONTACT
  ACTION DUDE AND ANDY RILEY

- PLUS: THE FAN GALLERY - SEND US
  YOUR OWN ACTION DUDE PICTURES,
  AND WE'LL PUT THE BEST ONES UP
  FOR THE WORLD TO SEE!

ABOUT THE AUTHOR

ANDY RILEY IS AN AUTHOR, A CARTOONIST AND A WRITER OF MOVIES AND TV.

HIS BOOKS INCLUDE THE *KING FLASHYPANTS* SERIES.

HIS TV AND FILM WRITING CREDITS INCLUDE *GNOMEO AND JULIET, HORRIBLE HISTORIES, RON'S GONE WRONG, THE PIRATES! IN AN ADVENTURE WITH SCIENTISTS,* AND THE BBC ADAPTATIONS OF DAVID WALLIAMS'S *GANGSTA GRANNY* AND *THE BOY IN THE DRESS.*

HERE COME THE CREDITS

EDITOR
FELICITY ALEXANDER

DESIGNER
MARGARET HOPE

WRITTEN AND DRAWN BY
ANDY RILEY

MISTER RILEY REPRESENTED BY
GORDON WISE
NIALL HARMAN